CORNWALL

JARROLD PUBLISHING, NORWICH

INTRODUCTION

Cornwall is almost an island. Except for its eastern border with Devon, it is surrounded by water – lashed by the mighty Atlantic on its northern shores, washed by the gentler English Channel to the south.

Cornwall's isolation from the rest of England and the dominance of the surrounding sea have helped to create its unique character, quite distinct from anywhere else in the country.

With no point further than twenty miles from the coast (only five miles separate Hayle on the Atlantic coast and Marazion in Mount's Bay), Cornwall was easier to reach by boat than by land until the middle of the nineteenth century. Then, in 1859, a new era dawned with the opening of Brunel's railway bridge over the River Tamar at Saltash.

The isolated peninsula was now linked to the rest of the country, and by the turn of the century had become a fashionable place to visit.

Today, tourism has largely replaced Cornwall's traditional industries such as tin-mining and fishing, and the region is one of the most popular English holiday resorts, attracting visitors from all over the world.

It is easy to see why. Cornwall's superb variety of breath-taking scenery alone is unrivalled. Along the north Cornwall coast, from Bude to Land's End, the surging Atlantic pounds against the spectacular cliffs, deep-sided valleys and miles of golden sand. Here are some of Europe's finest bathing and surfing beaches, of which Newquay is undoubtedly the most famous. In contrast, the Channel-facing south shores

offer a gentler perspective, with wooded hillsides, pretty fishing villages like Mevagissey and Polperro, and sheltered creeks ideal for small fishing boats and yachts. Land's End itself, England's most westerly point, is an awe-inspiring sight, where ocean meets channel and the sea is in constant turmoil. Inland, the wild, natural beauty of the moors, particularly Bodmin, presents yet another exceptional aspect of the Cornish landscape.

The surrounding sea also dominates the climate, with the warm gulf stream currents bringing extremely mild winters. Spring flowers appear earlier in Cornwall than anywhere else in Britain, and even sub-tropical species thrive in many of its gardens. Rare species of birds can be spotted too, attracted by the mild climate and the many estuaries and inlets along the 300-mile-long coastline.

Cornwall's unique heritage is another essential part of its attraction. From mysterious ancient stones to the King Arthur legend, and from nineteenth-century smuggling to Daphne du Maurier's *Jamaica Inn*, fact and fiction are inextricably intertwined. Steeped in mystery, legend and romance, Cornwall provides a rich source of inspiration for the imagination.

So, take time to explore Cornwall's magic: slow down to its rhythm of two tides a day like a true 'islander' and enjoy its very special charms.

THE LAND'S END PENINSULA

The Land's End or Penwith (Cornish for 'extreme end')
Peninsula stretches from near Godrevy Point and
Lighthouse on the north Atlantic coast to Prussia Cove
in the south.

The spectacular beauty of the landscape and the clarity
of light have long attracted artists to this region. There has
been an artist's colony at St Ives for nearly a hundred
years, with galleries and studios as much a local feature as
the fish cellars and shops. At Newlyn, adjoining Penzance,
Stanhope Forbes founded the famous school of artists at
the turn of the century.

On the south-facing side of the peninsula, between
the bustling harbour of Penzance and Land's End, are
various enchanting coves with romantic names like Porthcurno, Porthgwarra and Lamorno. In Mount's Bay, just off
Marazion, is the fairytale castle on St Michael's Mount,
approached by a causeway at low tide.

At Land's End itself, England's westernmost tip, there
are spectacular views all round, as well as exhibitions
and craftshops to visit. Nearby are the interesting rock
formations of Dr Syntax's Head, the Irish Lady and the
Armed Knight.

Numerous prehistoric stones, ruined clifftop fortresses
and disused tin mines throughout this area are eloquent
reminders of Cornwall's unique past.

Porthcurno's exquisite white sandy beach (**1**) is overlooked by the renowned open-air Minack Theatre, carved into the granite 200 ft above, and a breathtaking setting for a variety of productions each summer. There is fine walking country all around Cape Cornwall (**2**), Britain's only cape. (**3**) Craft workshops at Land's End. Penzance (**4**) is an excellent base for exploring the peninsula and the Scilly Isles.

4

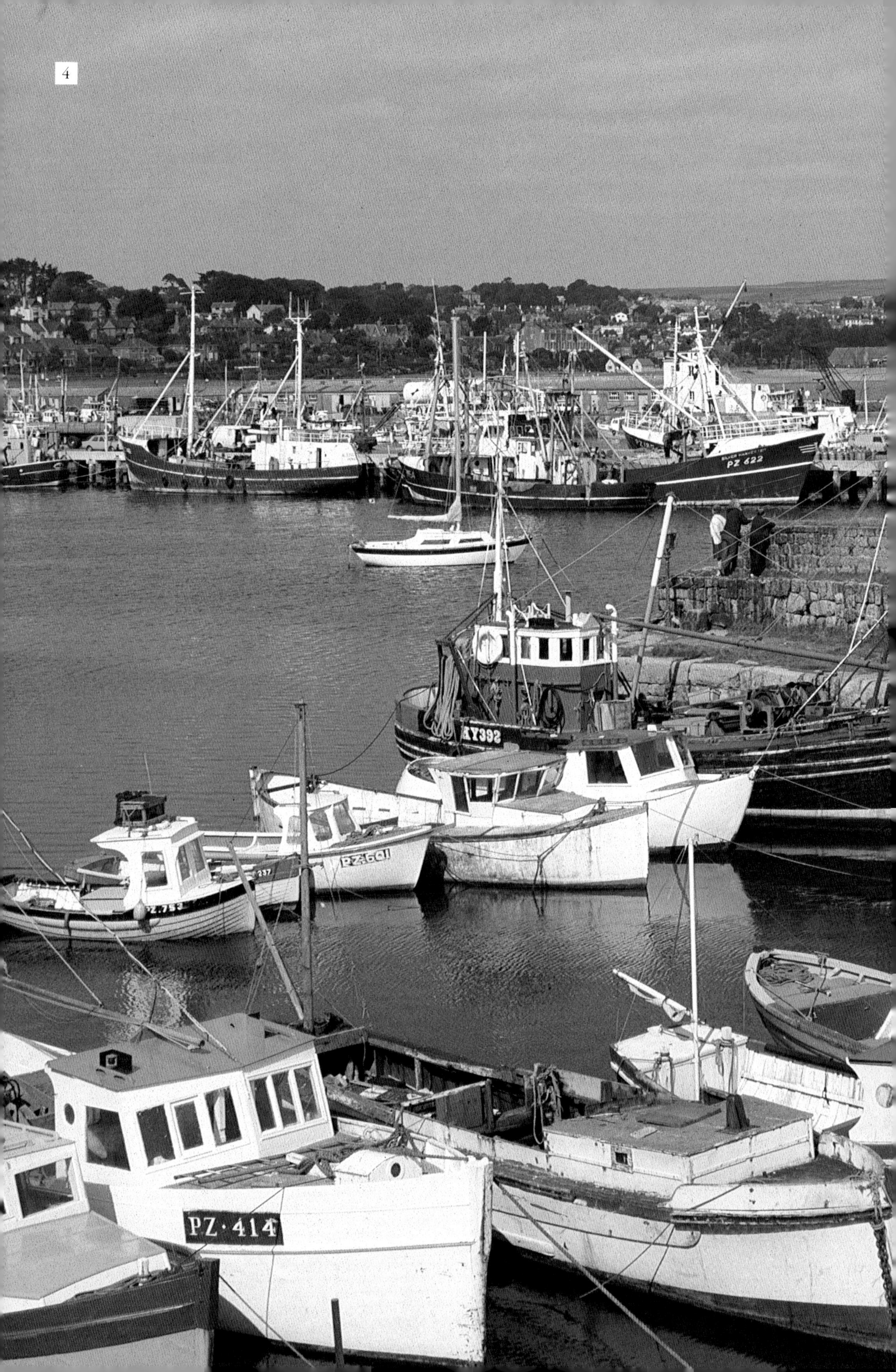

5

6

Just to the north of Land's End is the popular bathing and surfing beach at Sennen Cove (**5**). Porthgwarra (**6**) is one of the many delightful coves along the southern coast of the peninsula. Only ocean separates Land's End (**7**) and the USA. On a clear day, you can see the Longships and Wolf Rock lighthouses, where the sound of the wind whistling through the rocks used to torment the keepers.

St Ives (**8, 10**) is a busy fishing village with steep cobbled streets and closely-built houses surrounding the quayside. It is a well-established artist's colony, with numerous galleries, craft workshops, studios and museums. It is also the start of the Tinner's Way, a thirteen-mile track to Cape Cornwall, which follows an ancient trade route. Nearby, there are several excellent beaches, like the one at Porthminster (**9**).

12

11

Zennor (**11**) is an enchanting moorland village, situated west of St Ives on a magnificent stretch of the Cornwall Coast Path. D.H. Lawrence wrote *Women in Love* here. A bench-end in the twelfth-century church is carved with a mermaid, after a local legend. Newlyn (**12**) was formerly a pilchard-fishing centre, but is now mainly known for the Newlyn School of artists. (**13**) St Loy from Boscawen Point.

13

THE NORTH CORNWALL COAST

The north Cornwall coast presents a dramatic contrast
to the softer, more sheltered landscapes of the south.
The incredible Atlantic surf attracts thousands of visitors
each year in search of sun and sport, yet much of the
area remains unspoilt.

Boscastle was once an important port, despite a
difficult, winding entrance, enclosed by steep cliffs (**left**).
The sixteenth-century quay and picturesque cottages on
the hillside above make it one of Cornwall's most enchant
ing beauty spots. Its fourteenth-century Post Office is
owned by the National Trust, as is the harbour and
surrounding sea.

The cliffs of the north coast are the spring and summer
breeding-grounds for many species of birds, including the
delightful puffins who nest in their thousands at Lye Rock,
north of Tintagel, while river estuaries like the Camel and
the Hayle are particularly rich with birdlife during spring
and autumn migration. The coast is also noted for its
abundance of wild flowers, many of which are specially
adapted to cope with salt spray.

Newquay, Cornwall's most popular resort, attracts
holidaymakers of all types and ages, with its miles of
firm sand, magnificent surf, rock pools, caves and
clifftop walks.

Padstow (**14**) is an attractive fishing harbour on the Camel estuary.
It is the start of the ancient Saints' Way, which crosses the Cornish
peninsula to Fowey on the south coast, re-tracing the route of
the early Celtic missionaries. Newquay (**15**) is without doubt
Cornwall's premier holiday resort, and a major surfing centre.
(The World Championships were held here in 1987.)

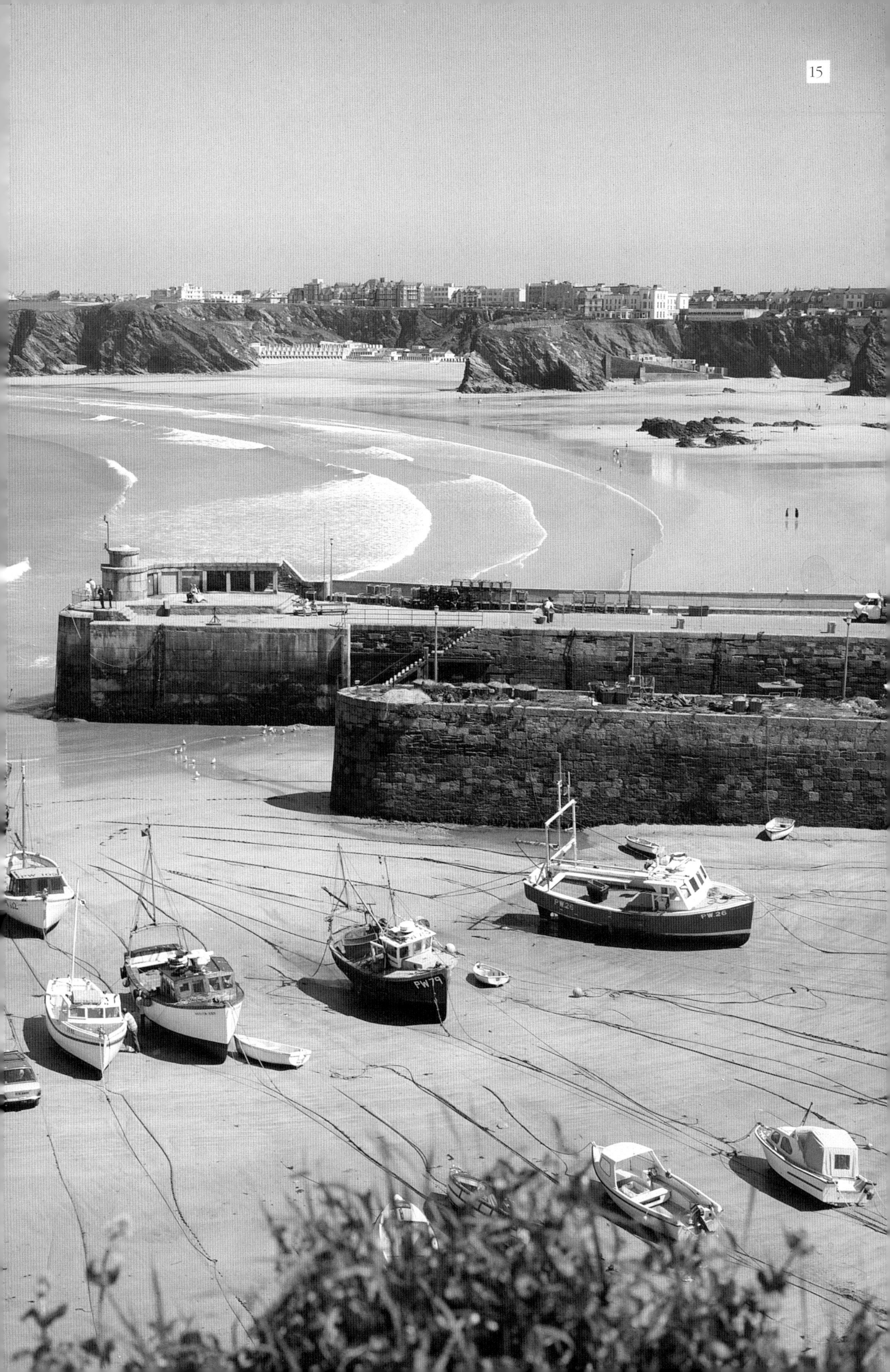
PW 26
PW 26
PW79

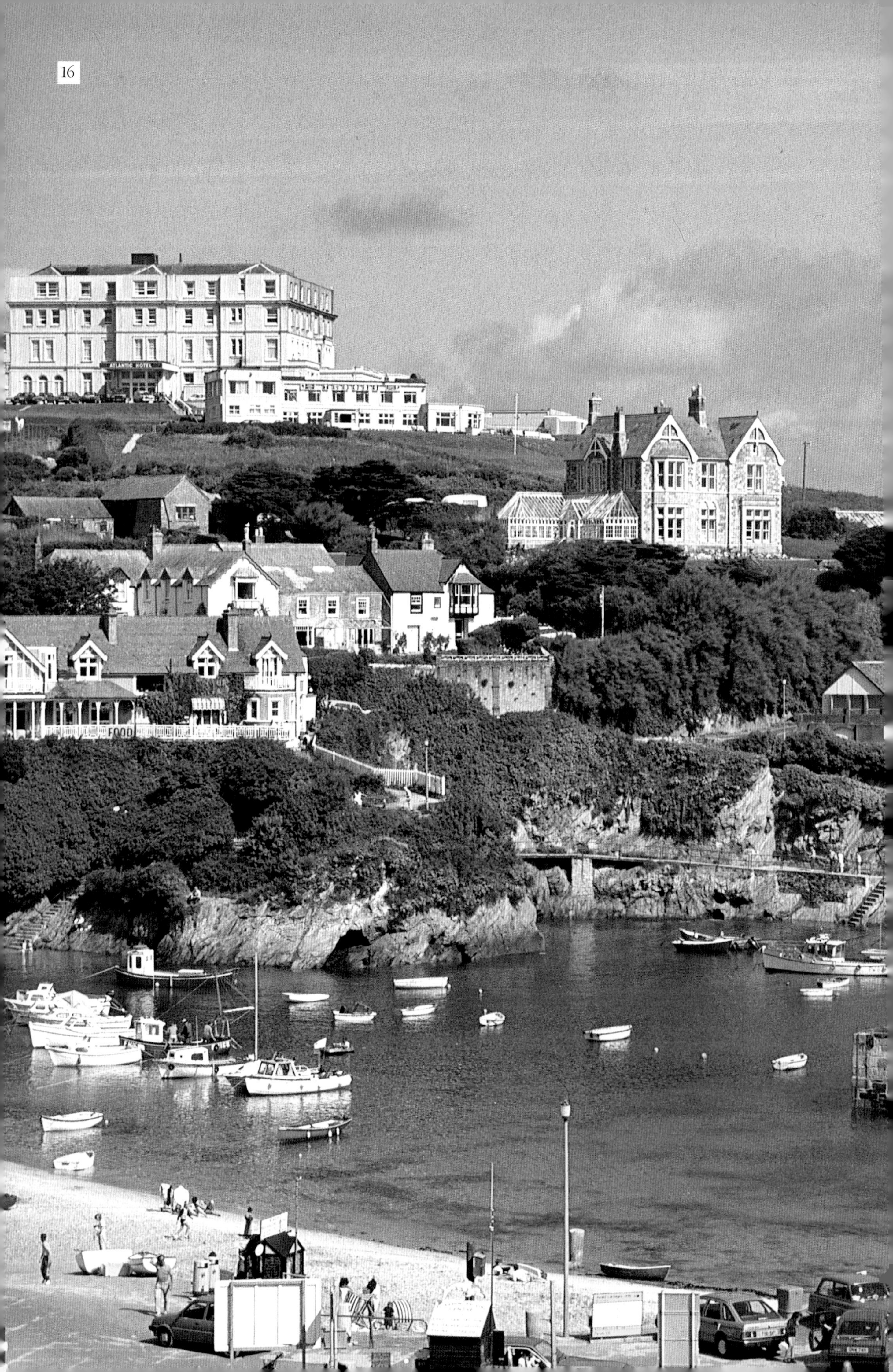
ATLANTIC HOTEL
FOOD

(**19**) Holywell Bay, famous for its towering sand dunes.
(**20**) Trevone Bay, near Padstow. Once a busy port, Bude (**21**)
today is a spacious resort with huge sandy beaches and excellent
surfing. Trebarwith Strand (**22**) lies two miles south of Tintagel.
It has a popular beach, and a gentle stretch of the Cornwall Coast
Path runs along its clifftops.

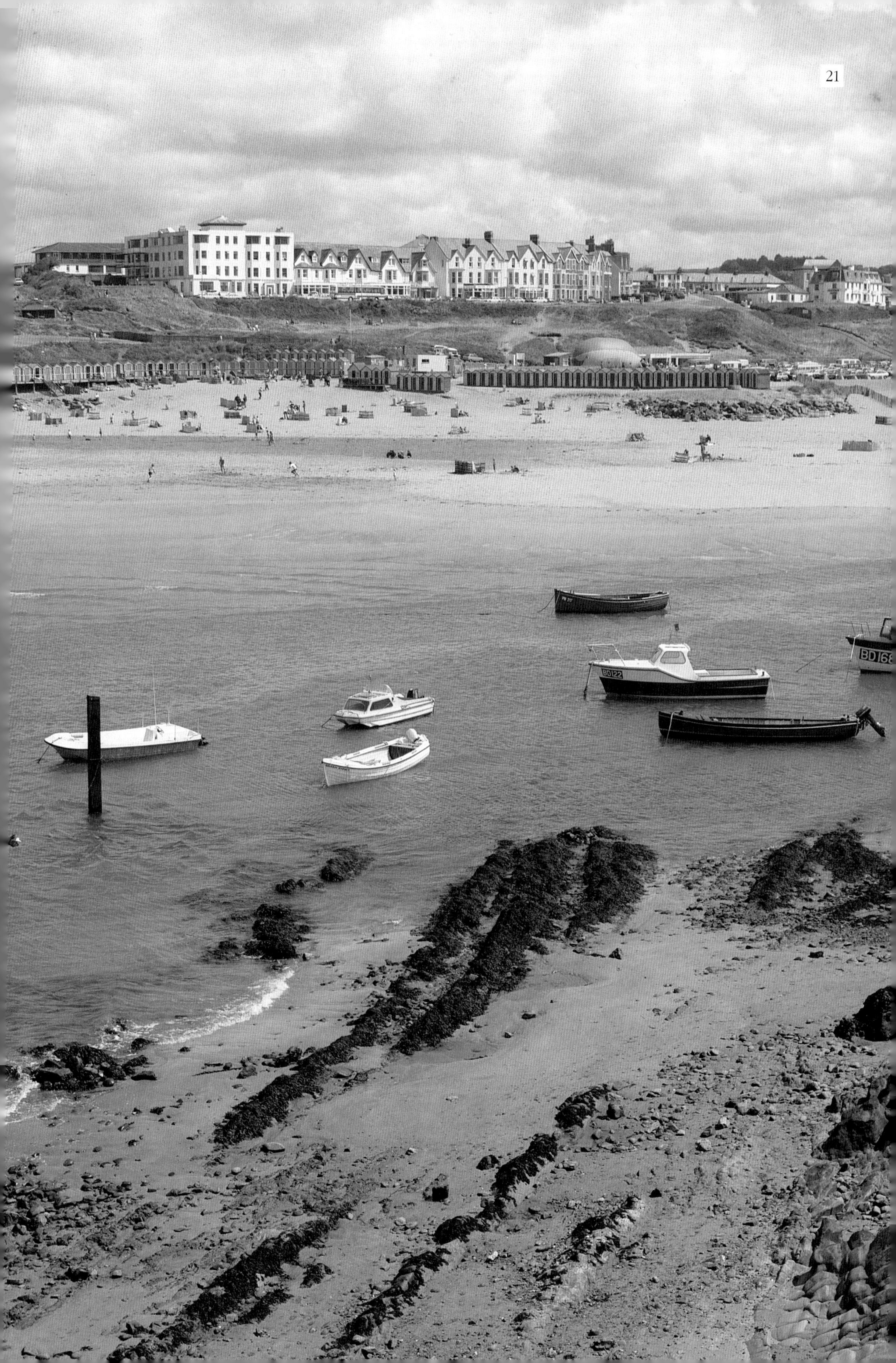
BD122

Portreath (**23**), west of St Agnes, was built in the eighteenth
century for the export of copper. Port Isaac (**24**) has been a fishing
harbour since the Middle Ages, and is characterised by its fish
cellars, narrow streets and geranium-filled alleyways. The Long
Cross Victorian Gardens lie within sight of the Atlantic at Port
Isaac and are based on a former Victorian layout, with steps, water,
rockeries and shrubs. (**25**) Towan Head, near Newquay.

THE SOUTH CORNWALL COAST

Cornwall's south coast is sometimes called the 'Cornish Riviera' because of its mild climate, luxuriant flora, and attractive resorts.

The white-washed cottages perched on the wooded hillsides above Mevagissey and Polperro give these picturesque fishing ports a distinctly Continental air.

Their harbours are the two most photographed in Cornwall, but tourism has not totally replaced the traditional fishing industries. The closely-built houses on the quayside once made excellent hiding-places for smugglers and contraband.

Looe, **below**, is another harbour reminiscent of the

Mediterranean, with its long estuary, wooded slopes, and tree-covered cliffs.

The south coast's numerous sheltered creeks and estuaries have provided a safe haven for generations of fishermen and sailors. Falmouth's maritime tradition goes back to the days of Post Office packets, and it is said to be the world's third largest natural harbour.

Fowey also has a seafaring tradition. Few buildings on the quayside main street have changed since Sir Francis Drake's time. Fowey's marvellous natural harbour has made it one of Britain's finest sailing centres, with vessels of every shape and size in the wooded estuary.

Kynance Cove (**26, 27**) lies north-east of Lizard village, and is perhaps the most enchanting of the Cornish coves. Kynance means 'ravine' in Cornish, and all around there are interesting rock formations, brilliantly coloured serpentine rock, and blow holes that roar like cannons. Its fine sand and timeless beauty attract crowds in the summer, even though the descent from the clifftops is steep.

Looe (**28**) is really two towns in one, East and West Looe, linked by
a celebrated seven-arched bridge. The long River Looe estuary is a
haven for small fishing boats and yachts, and the area is the British
centre for shark-fishing. Polperro (**29**) is perhaps Cornwall's most
picturesque fishing village, tightly wedged in a cleft in the cliffs.
The Smugglers' Museum recreates the town's smuggling history.

Pendower Beach (**30**) in Gerrans Bay, Roseland, is extensive and rarely crowded. Roseland itself is a charming and largely undiscovered part of Cornwall. The Lizard (**31**) is not Britain's most southerly point (nearby Polpeor Cove is), but it is a paradise for botanists, with twenty rare plant species in the area. Inland, Goonhilly Downs is the site of the British Telecom Earth Satellite Station. (**32**) View from Gribbin Head. (**33**) Polruan, near Fowey.

34

(**34**) St Mawes Castle. (**35**) Coverack, a former smugglers' haunt. Despite its chocolate-box charm, Mevagissey (**36**) is the largest fishing port in St Austell's Bay. The attractive port of St Mawes (**37**) on the Roseland peninsula is linked to Falmouth (**38**) by ferry. Falmouth developed as a port when Sir Walter Raleigh realised the potential of the Carrick Roads as a huge deep-water anchorage. (**39**) Charlestown, near St Austell.

35

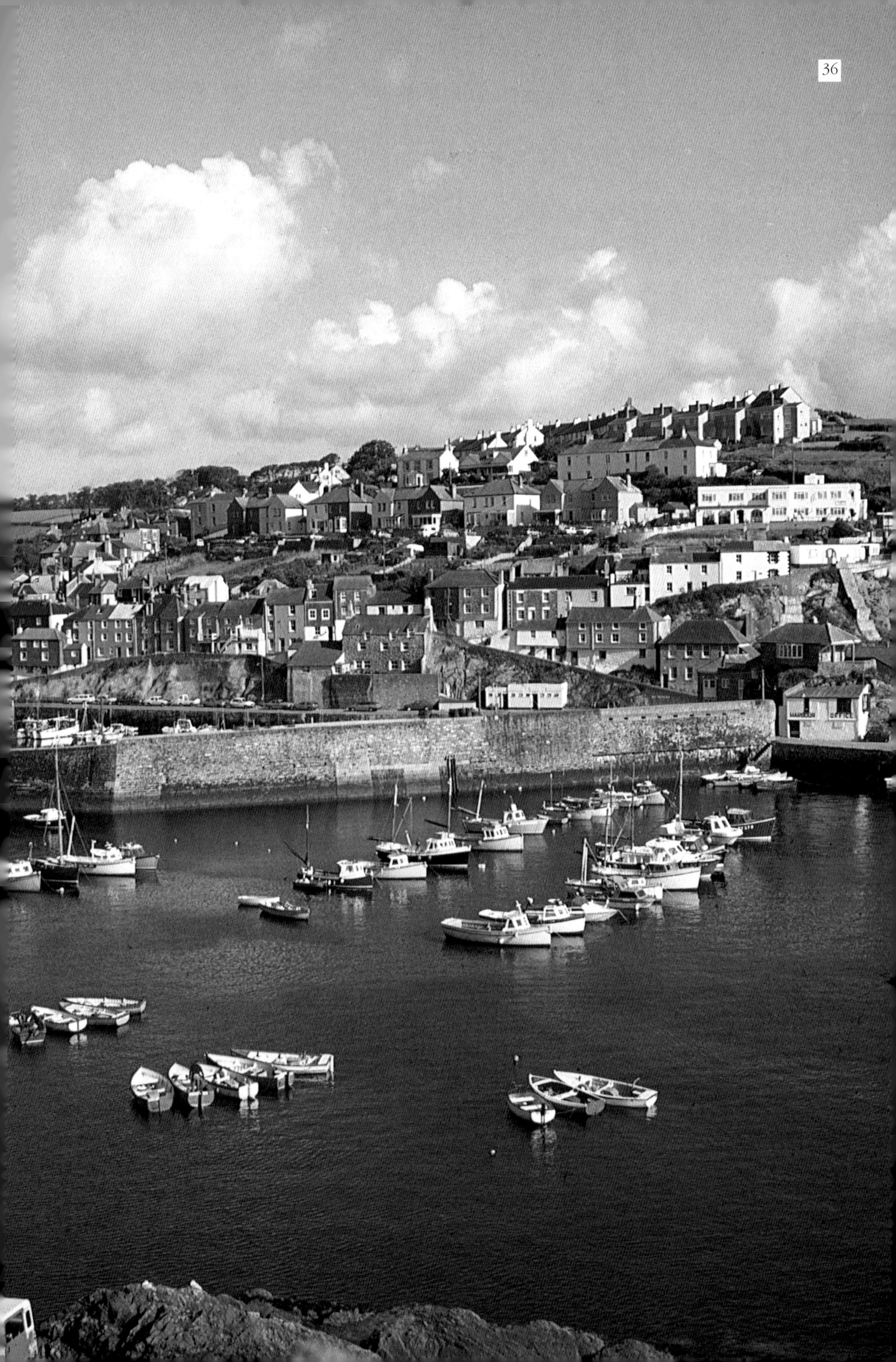
HARBOUR OFFICE

CORNWALL'S HERITAGE

Cornwall is richly endowed with relics of its ancient and not-so-distant past.

There are numerous burial mounds, stone circles, Iron-Age settlements and other antiquities which bear witness to Cornwall's early visitors. Many are in a good state of preservation, particularly those on the Penwith Peninsula and Bodmin Moor, because Cornwall has never been heavily industrialised.

Other clues to Cornwall's heritage are in its place names and local surnames. For example, St Neot, St Agnes, (St) Austell and Padstow (after St Petroc), are named after the Celtic missionaries who landed in Cornwall in the sixth and seventh centuries. Common prefixes such as pen- (headland), porth- (harbour) and tre- (settlement) reveal this Celtic influence, as Cornwall developed its own language and customs in isolation from the rest of the country. An old rhyme illustrates this:

By Tre, Ros, Pol, Lan, Car and Pen
Ye shall know most Cornishmen

The present-day Cornish landscape is dotted with gaunt chimney stacks emerging from ruined engine-houses, like the one on Bodmin Moor pictured **below**, indicating the demise of the local tin-mining industry. Cheaper production methods abroad gradually forced the closure of many Cornish mines in the nineteenth century.

The influence of the surrounding sea is obvious in the numerous picturesque fishing ports and former smugglers' coves which punctuate the coast. The Cornwall Coast Path (272 miles long) embraces many other characteristic features of Cornwall's heritage, including prehistoric monuments, medieval churches, castles and historic houses.

40

41

The Cheesewring (**40**) on Bodmin Moor is a natural phenomenon, but the Hurlers (**43**), also on Bodmin, date from 2000 BC and were probably the site of a pagan ritual. Tintagel has traditionally been associated with the King Arthur legend, although the castle (**41**), said to have been Arthur's, is now only a romantic clifftop ruin. Truro (**42**) is Cornwall's 'capital' as county administrative centre and cathedral city.

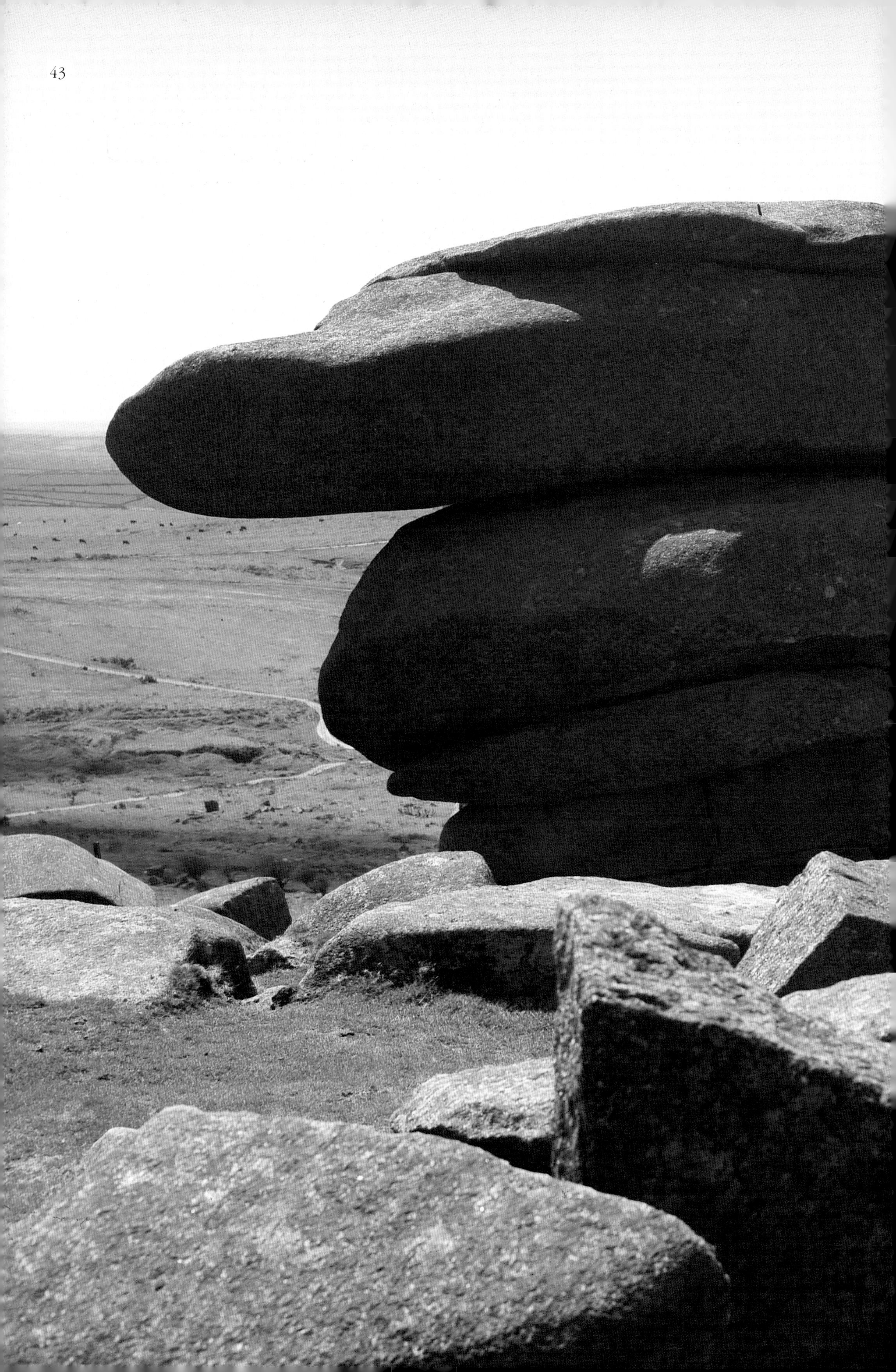

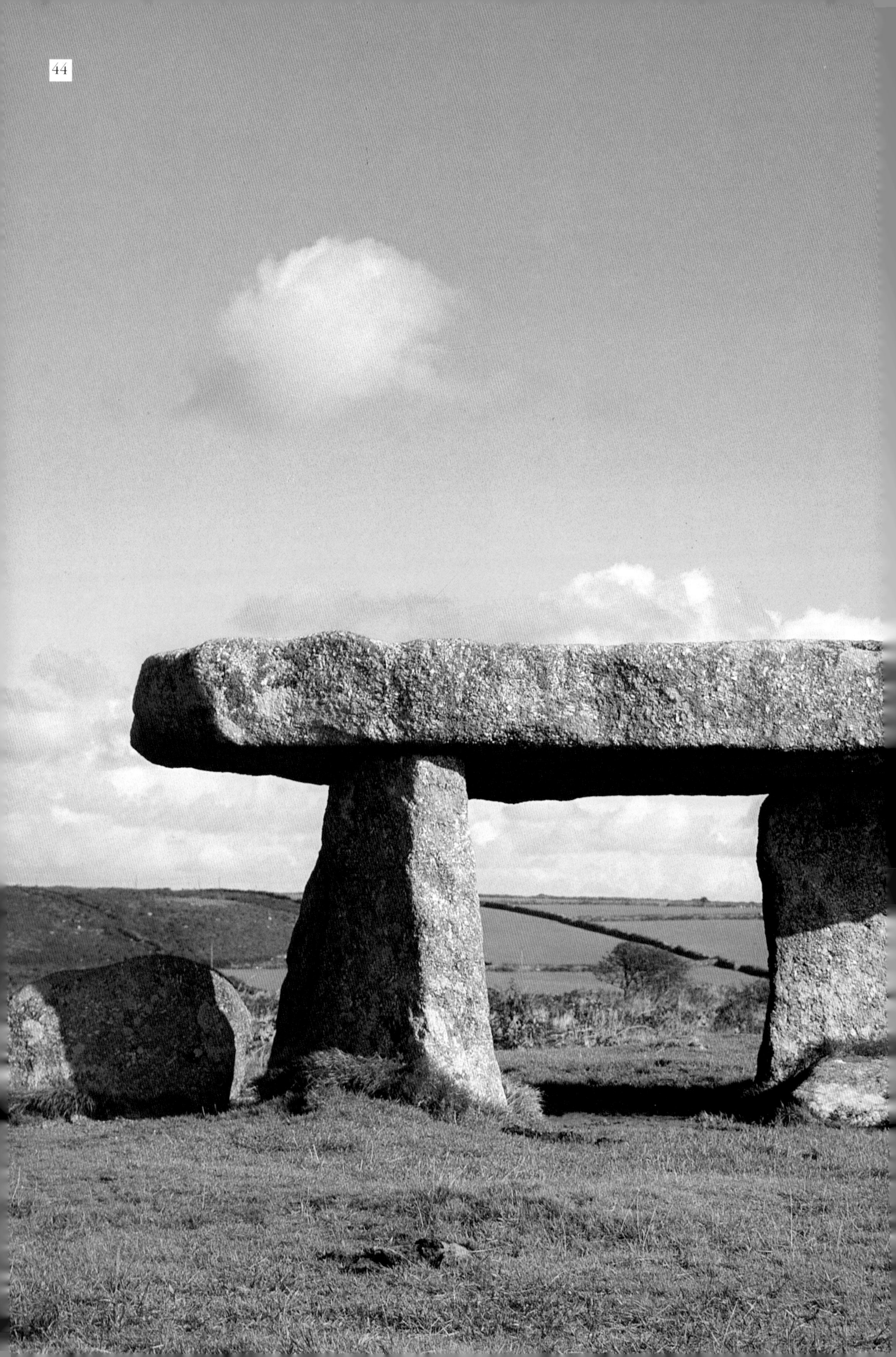

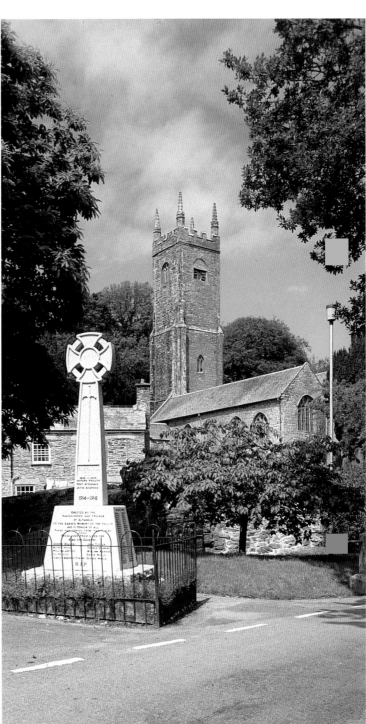

Lanyon Quoit (**44**), near Madron on the Land's End Peninsula, dates from the Neolithic era and was built originally as a tomb, with two huge upright granite slabs supporting a capstone or 'quoit', like a card-house. These were then covered in a mound of earth and stones. (**45**) Church at Altarnun, near Bodmin Moor. The majority of Cornish churches were built in the Middle Ages by a variety of benefactors including nobility, landed gentry and merchants.

46

47

Mystery and legend surround Cornwall's history. Bodmin Moor
(**46**) is the site of Dozmary Pool, whose deep still waters are said
to be the resting-place of King Arthur's sword Excalibur. The Royal
Albert Bridge (**47**), at Saltash over the River Tamar, linked Cornwall
with the rest of England when it opened in 1859. (**48**) St Levan's
Stone, near Porthcurno.

49

(**49**) The Huer's House on the clifftop at Newquay. The 'huer'
used to alert the local community to the coming of the huge pil-
chard shoals in the eighteenth and nineteenth centuries, indicated
by a reddish streak in the sea. Cornwall has many beautiful historic
houses and gardens, such as Cotehele House, near Callington (**50**),
Lanhydrock House (N.T.) near Bodmin (**51**), and Trelissick
Gardens (**52**). (**53**) Towanroath Shaft, Wheal Cote Mine,
St Agnes (N.T.).

50

Front cover: Land's End
Title page: Boats at Mevagissey
Back cover: St Michael's Mount

Text by Bernadette Sheehan
ISBN 0·7117·0508·9
© Jarrold Publishing 1990
Published by Jarrold Publishing, Norwich. Printed in Great Britain. 1/90

Picture credits
Terry Harber: title page; Cathie Welchman: introduction; Colour Library Books Ltd:
aerial view of Land's End, (**10**), (**25**); Roy J. Westlake, A.R.P.S.: (**3**), (**15**), (**18**),
(**20**), (**23**), (**24**), (**30**), (**36**), (**37**), (**52**); A. Cave: (**21**); J.C. Ticehurst: (**22**), (**28**),
(**33**), (**39**), (**43**), (**47**); Cornwall Tourist Board: (**27**); Charles A. Brown: (**38**);
A.S. Greaves: (**53**).